Crossing the

Julian Turner
Crossing the Outskirts

ANVIL PRESS POETRY

Published in 2002
by Anvil Press Poetry Ltd
Neptune House 70 Royal Hill London SE10 8RF
www.anvilpresspoetry.com

ISBN 0 85646 352 3

This book is published
with financial assistance from
The Arts Council of England

A catalogue record for this book
is available from the British Library

Designed and set in Monotype Janson by Anvil
Printed and bound in England
by Cromwell Press, Trowbridge, Wiltshire

And some there be, which have no memorial; who are perished, as though they had never been . . . and their children after them. But these were merciful men, whose righteousness hath not been forgotten.

ECCLESIASTICUS XLIV.9–10

Acknowledgements

Acknowledgements are due to the following, where some of these poems first appeared:

boomerang.com: 'Eclogue' (as 'Against Flowers') and 'The 1963 Clarendon Press Atlas of Britain and Northern Ireland'
Poetry London: 'The Director's Cut', 'Penalty of Stroke and Distance' and 'The Seal People'
The Reater: 'The Magnificent History of the English'
The Rialto: 'Reportage' and 'Tennis Ball'

'Livery' was published in *The Ring of Words*, the 1998 Arvon International Poetry Competition publication. 'The Seal People' was included in *Loanwords*: poetry and etchings, an art box, with Alison Rouse, 1999. 'Whale Bone' was awarded first prize in the 1993 Northwords poetry competition.

Contents

Crossing the Outskirts

The Start of Something New

My mother's grave – the priests drunk
and hurrying to have it done,
the coffin jostled down
before I get there breathless,
the hymns half sung, lost
to sky with its always open doors.

These last few days a dream –
her eyes like pike below
the lake-ice of morphine;
her long, muttering sleeps
and sudden conversation;
on Friday, sitting there,
propped up by nurses beforehand,
as empty as the air;

and now over the hedges, their white floss
of smiling blossoms, a figure
with my mother's hair
beginning her waiting game.

The 1963 Clarendon Press Atlas of Britain and Northern Ireland

Read here the total sheep in 1955:
23,037,015;
the landings of hake, turbot and sole that year;
the exact distribution of clover, sainfoin, lucerne,
the temporary grasses; the number of factories
built over a 10-year period, each pie-chart
proving we *never had it so good.*

An ex-book now and stamped DISCARDED,
it draws a section through this old century
illustrating the world into which I was born –
the coppice and High Forest acreage of elm,
the gross tonnage of coal, miles of wire,
the casting houses of finished steel and tin-plate;
industries on the verge of technology's *white heat*
and coming meltdown; the estimated yield
of littoral seaweed; a time of thick, black flex
in love with itself, its facts and shabby streets
whose pavements danced with jewels of mica-frost.

The last plate (Submarine and Coastal Relief)
shows the old country perched precarious
on Europe's shoulder in a pool of light,
the underwater features inked in black,
their postscript epitaph a lullaby:
Beaufort's Dyke and Raithlin Sound,
Sule Sgeir Bank and Fladen Ground,
the Devil's Hole, the Broad Fourteens,

Outer Silver Pit, Clay Deep,
the Sovereign Shoals and Buttock Bank;
nomenclature where knowledge peters out,
transporting me from shelves and Dewey system
to the dark blue of unnamed, unnumbered contours.

Glider Pilot

I used to try to make him say he'd killed
some Germans, taken sniper fire or stood
beside some damaged Horsa while he thrilled
to shrapnel, tracer, blood. He never would.

He didn't want to marry in the war.
He watched the ones who did change from a high,
cold arrogance which stood above the law
of chance, to caution, take one step and die.

A gambler's instinct. This would help him down
to earth by scrolling pictures as he flew
sightlessly over strange and blacked-out towns
to drop behind the lines his wrecking crew.

Beforehand, all men were confined to base:
killing and lust informed their stratagems.
They'd shag whatever in their wooden crates.
The Top Brass hand-picked WAAFs to service them.

Love sometimes rooted, though, above the mess
where thirsts were slaked and loneliness expressed
in drunken blazes. The tortured will confess
with lips apart beside a pale breast.

She worked the bar. He noticed how she picked
her way between the lewd remarks. Her brown
hair shone on evening flights, the tarmac licked
its long tongue out for him as he came down.

The operation morning came. They said
goodbyes with eye-lash kisses, knowing they
might never meet again. The prop-wind dragged
the tow. A dust-cloud carried him away.

They did meet once, when dust had died and war
was done. Her village glistened under rain,
the blackened terraces and slag hills where
she wheeled her son. He did not come again.

The weary will refuse a lonely road.
He married someone soft, was true in this
at least: was not in love with her, he said;
worked hard; had children which he knew were his.

Grenade-blast fragments in his fingers burnt
like memories. My mum would keep at bay,
by scrubbing me with energy that hurt,
the sense of something pulling him away.

Penalty of Stroke and Distance

These are the ones whose rules, exact and pure,
remind you poor conditions are no excuse;
who in all weathers will turn out and draw
their pitching irons cold from rusted pools,
who practise after dark their follow-through,
their swing-weight, wrist cock and pre-putt routine
alone with fog or rain in motley shoes
like shadows on the ninth at Hallowe'en.

Have you seen them when snow has turned the links
into a glittercloth of blinding stymies?
Then they cut loose, lost on the fairway banks,
intent and abstract, caddying their dead ponies
through waistdeep drifts across Antarctica.
They shield their faces from the icy sun
in search of pitchmarks on a glacier,
in search of the most extreme hole-in-one.

You must have seen them, in the dead afternoon
returning with their far-off eyes, as touched
as if their untried souls had journeyed on,
the long climb over and their summit reached,
their parka hoods on fire; forgotten ones
who stumble home, their hair as white as snow,
to strangeness at the heart of what they know,
uncomprehending faces, eyes that shun.

Livery

At the last count there were 329 members
of the Bassett-Lowke Newsletter – cognoscenti
of 'O' gauge model railways, not just any
old locomotives, rolling stock or tenders;
these are as exact as what they represent:
a four-wheeled tin-plate Brake Van (vgc),
an Exley blood and custard coach (with seats),
a boxed-up Standard Scale 'Pacific' (mint).

Those in the know can read between the lines:
a pre-war world that smells of oil and steam,
where ladies made of lead wait on the platform
with their hat-boxes and ask porters the time.
Each figure has its own stand and station,
each knows the proper form – how to address
the other, bearing in mind their rank and class,
the correct way to convey correct information.

The badly Xeroxed text is smudged but true,
a recipe for what the real world lacks –
the signal certainty of shining tracks
which reach beyond horizons where the new
threatens like thunderheads. The Bassett-Lowkies
tidy their layouts, while outside the blur
of the world hangs like painted sack and loofah
against matt duck-egg blue of hardboard skies.

Bert Haines' Yard

What was it my dad and brother were searching for,
those times they dragged me down to Bert Haines' yard,
thistles and groundsel bushing up through floors
of cars, the unhinged gravestones of van doors
tilting towards the sun, their paintwork scarred
by unrecorded bumps and scrapes, a ghost
topography where all things come to rest,

the stripped down bicycles and engine parts,
vast sprockets from the giants' industries,
their magnitude remembering lost arts
of universes smelted and cast in foundries
moving at night to patterns planned by star-charts,
an after-life of objects grassed in dust
and grease, a leaf-soft mall which sells what's lost,

forgotten, repossessed, passed on: cement
statues, wheel-less wheelbarrows, old machines,
their movements gone? Maybe some link between
two boyhoods, a chain broken by accident
which they must mend but didn't have the means?
To find among the litter of the dead
a golden circlip? Neither ever said.

Tennis Ball

All things have gravity – its universal
principle makes Earth come up to meet
a tennis ball; the lover bearing down
provokes a rise; the rails push up against
the train and parachutists spread themselves
like fingers on a fountain-flail of air
until their ribbon snakes up to the clouds;
fledglings fall from nests to find their wings;
a foal is dropped and climbs on to his feet;
the Fall implies a faith in being caught.
Such things have weight.
Jane tied a brief knot in a nylon rope,
climbed up into an open loft and dipped,
a swallow from a wire.

The Magnificent History of the English

My aunt has racked up blade bone steak for tea,
her gravy thick with atavistic freight.
She stands in strip-light clenching and unclenching
her freckled, arthritic hands on kitchen air.

Together, we have trawled through the photo albums
and found Ida – the great aunt I remember
fluttering in her chair beside the fire
in Hitchin, frail, her hands afraid like birds.

But in these tiny snaps she's young again,
even happy-looking. Here she is with Bud –
her pet name for my aunt – her rusty, damaged
blade of a face suddenly lit from within.

She was how my aunt survived the cold
touch of her own mother who only saw her son,
who lavished love on him, the boast of Arlesey
at her bridge parties, and who gave her none.

Towards the end of Ida's album Tom
appears; his bland disguise of tennis whites
conceals his marriedness, the way he had
her in the potting shed, the fists of his knees,

and other men: the Revd. Knightly in
the bucket seat of 'the good old Morris Cowley',
tennis with doctors from the loony bin,
and Cecil Soundry shaving in his vest.

On the inside back cover Bud stands
squinting up at the sun. She holds a wand
of bracken. With her other arm she looks
for Ida who bends down to fill her hand.

My aunt carries out the bones. She locks
the door on distant memory with relief.
We both look down the long corridor, and laugh
at the fucked Turners, English as roast beef.

Eclogue

Sowbane, Bogwort, Bugloss, Toadflax and Forget-me-not:
it will be the detritus of these that I scrape from my boots
    at dusk,
coming home from the valley decked out like Florizel, slightly
perspiring, having pitched the fury of my feet against all manner
of harmless thing, against the pert, cross-clashing blades
    of grass,
their lethal edges steel in the glistening dew, against the dreamy
    stars
of wild garlic floating in the forest's deep twilight, small boats
upon a sea in which all nightmares lurk, against the innocent
    and mild,
the mindless daffodil, the insulting abundance of the buttercup,
the ox-eye's wink, the retributive, infuriating non-amnesia
    of poppies,
against even leaf-mould and the lichens whose modest
    encrustations
have taken centuries to build, simply because of their close
    kinship,
in short, against everything which reminds me of you.
And if we must communicate, we will do so through *Interfauna*.

White Herd

As Lilith walks the wilderness in storms,
or flame-tongues wrap around a schooner's mast
to tell the sailors that the worst has passed
when fury rolls the sea to mammoth forms,
they graze the city's rim, their souls revealed.
Where the last semi crumbles, streets mutate
to tracks and gardens are lank, uncouth, they wait –
forty-five splinters of light in their own field.

They call down from the sky its paler mass
and glow with it. They are the boundary stones
which mark our limits, guarding where white bones
lie deep below the thresholds all must pass.
We pass them each way, to and home from work;
do not look up or notice them with pain
in rear-view mirrors smudged and smeared with rain.
Wildfire in fields. Lit windows in the dark.

Daphnis and Chloë

How many hundred years did blossoms flower
under her feet which hardly touched the ground,
when we were kissing by the bearded pond?
How I must have wanted, wanted her.

Now darkness, blight and fog as thick as wool,
the farms smoking in half-light, her on her own
crossing the outskirts of this dormitory town,
the collar of her fleece turned up. Wistful.

Next to the tarmac bays where vans arrive
I've watched her in her leather kecks, with carters
and milk-boys, still wearing the wilderness
as mud and straw-dung dried upon her sleeve,

as haw berries and forgetfulness of fields;
their faces flushed like our old dawns, their cabs
steamed up, their engines editing her sobs
in that morning light when bruises are revealed,

and I have tried to tell her how it feels
to watch and say nothing, followed her beyond
the town to her lair, to touch her, to remind
her, but the air swallowed the sound of her heels.

All stories, even ours, must have an end
and so I've left the others with our sheep –
I tail her past the bus station, the butchers' shop,
the chained Netto trolleys, over the waste ground,

its razor wire and intruder lights. The chase
ends here, in the alleys by the slaughterhouse.
She turns to me at bay, but amorous.
There is so little left to sacrifice.

Walk-On Parts

The model shop on the Lindow road out of Wilmslow,
where we bought dowelling, fuse-wire, metal rings
for restraining sails,
varnish for the hulls, from here it wasn't far

to where the common's brush scrub and coal earth
scowled at our knees.
The lake was a wound of light on a dark ground
but shallow, unexpressive as dead eyes seemed

before they were ballasted with black pennies.
The yachts were brave.
They chased each other against the grain of waves,
racing, their red sails pointing at the clouds.

They found her after we had moved away,
the stake of oak which anchored her worked loose,
but in my mind
I saw her rise slowly from the black water,

her hair pulled out like stuffing from a seat,
a torque of wire plaited round her neck,
her bones dissolved,
and staring with those eyes bright as her rings.

Her soul gave the place we knelt to set sail
its permanent mood,
the gloom of broken willows, low unwilling
clouds, the splintered echelons of geese.

Leg the Dentist

All pain is finite, dentists say.
My room-sized tongue is pinned by her
spare thumb. She tamps down drums of clay
and cotton-wool. I ng and urr.

Her bone-white fingers rummage in
the soft soil of my face, poking
down for Yorick with a tiny
fork and spade, and she's not joking

as she banters with the nurse,
who reads me like a haruspex.
She leans on me, her rose lips pursed.
You only get this close in sex:

I'll pay for this. The hole half-dug,
she muses gravely what to do
while we can both hear drifting up
through silence, Hell's Radio 2.

Caducous

Soon after she ditched my brother for a dentist,
she took off to start a Jesus magazine
with weeping text and hippy Letraset,
italics choking sense in every line.

This publication introduced me to
the word *caducous* – ugly as a sin
I thought, and saw her flare as candles do,
first lithe and briefly lit by passion,   ,

then a drizzled stub. That January
they invited me to their low cottage where
the wide slope of the vale dipped to the Wye
and a bare oak gripped the ground in its vast claw.

I sat in front of her and played guitar
badly, in half-light, while those lamp-black eyes
burned with reflections of the open fire
and a darker flame I didn't recognise.

I was fifteen and into Jesus too.
I wrote a love song to them both. I heard
it first walking in the valley, put a few
raggedy, uneven chords to its poor words

and sang it out of key. But I still see
what I saw then – winter-lit ochres, the edge
of distant copses scumbled with verdigris,
a bustling wren ebullient in a hedge,

instant energy I could breathe in, the ache
of empty blue, or old leaves in a pond,
their veins of indigo and crimson lake,
the little worlds of dew on each fern frond.

This was the first wish – to look below
the fleeting at the underlying shades,
the roots from which the rules of order grow,
and glory in the rainbow while it fades.

I looked for their house yesterday; the hamlet
sprawled round the oak, its orchards, tortured eaves,
careless, untutored gardens. I couldn't find it –
all the house-names had changed, all trace of lives

before brushed from the floors, the ghost patchouli
candles snuffed, dhoop-sticks of dark rooms gone,
as if the land had lost its memory.
The valley shivered in the setting sun.

Do we smell? she asked. She couldn't tell,
it seemed, because they spent all day naked,
and the sweat of sudden prayer took its toll.
I tried to put the thought out of my head,

them kneeling on the steep stairs having sex:
two differently intoxicating fervours,
which imply a third when they are mixed.
Any smell becomes you, I assured her.

Scarecrow Hospital

At visiting time the birds descend on us
to haunt us with their twittering for food.
We stand propped up against the walls, the piss
pasting our rags against our knotted wood.
I do not think I know who these souls are,
who sing inside the sackcloth of our heads.
They steal our starbursts of unruly hair.
Our shoulders wear the dandruff of their seeds.

Uprooted, there is nothing left to fear.
Finally free to dream of freedom's birds
we echo them. They scare us with desires,
their broken music which cannot be heard.
I pity them their friendlessness, their rare
and immaterial touch, their ghostly waul
which drifts down some forgotten corridor.
I call them to me through the hospital.

How frightening we are we are not told.
The nurses tut and rearrange our straw.
The food they give us flattens everything –
the sheets, horizons, slug-shapes on the floor
through which I glimpse the sky, its hawks of gold
hanging on fire above the silent snow.
My empty head is filled with whispering.
There's something of this I will never know.

Reading Paul Nash

Coming home from his own war he washed up
at Dymchurch, drew the ghost of himself alone,
an afterthought transparent on the prom,
the unremitting waters full of ill-
defined and broken things in monochrome.

His *Night Tide* brought the dead back bone by bone.
He knew how badly we are made, where
the stress fractures are, how we maim what we love,
why the wreckage haunts: he had emptied the Somme
of bodies, filled it with a light that hurt.

Later he met Eileen Agar in Swanage.
She turned his sea to something blue again
briefly. From then he watched where they had been –
in the high skies, freewheeling, the vapour trails
a signature of some lost faculty.

The world is full of things that come to this:
the rib-cage fuselage, the flat-fish wings
like spatulas, the shark fins of metal waves,
the wreckage, blistered paint and lonely wheels –
the place where dreams of flight are put to sleep.

He was dying as the visions spooled away.
He watched her in her letters, naked, far off,
almost human, but the old tide had come in
wiping away the driftwood she had brought him,
that smile of hers, his strong jaw in the sun.

Knowing the Ropes

I'm thinking of a rope, how it's made.
A walker serves his rope against the lay:
the fibres first are twisted into yarns,
each filament then spun against its turns
to cords, cords into strands, or readies, which
determine by their twist degrees of stretch.
The turning of the units is the trick:
the Victory's anchor rope was two feet thick,
a hundred fathoms long and weighed twelve ton;
a galleon had 15 miles of rigging on.
Even a harvester will rope the top bale
down to the rick with straw spun on a whimbel.

All of us trust our lives to them: in lifts
their loops and lifelines spool in sooty shafts –
they hide their cable work from worried eyes;
we move like silk between the streets and skies.
The morning hawsers on the tower cranes
shine in the wind, their payloads of machines
weightless above the swarming building site.
My father's Horsa on the outward flight
to Arnhem grew a tow-rope ball of hemp
so huge he had to leave formation, and limp
home; his replacement took a direct hit.
All personnel were lost above Utrecht.

St Catherine of Alexandria's
the virgin patron saint of rope-makers.
Maximinus the Second had her roped
on to a spiked wheel and then beheaded.
It's said that people snap and cannot mend.
Are humans less strong than a rope of sand?

The Director's Cut

The hands that hold the knife are not my own.
The way the flesh peels back like parted lips,
the way the walls of tissue raspberry-ripple,
sudden shocks of rush in little sips,
the pinching of the skin to stem the blood,
the numbness spreading through the musculature,
the way the knife lies by the plate of toast,
the linen dressings creamy, clean and sure;

like being in a fight with no one else,
exact and under my control, the tense
build-up, the downjerk of the hand, the surge
of quick relief; the stupid, dull attempts
to mend it; wet, red cloths, the winding round
of bandages; the hush. All these make sense.

How the Manticore was Made

Older than Hell this pictured bestiary
and we part-serpent in our lidless eyes,
cold-bloodedness and guile, part general brute
distinguished from them only by our thumb
and poor excuses for a life that's nine-
tenths numb, one tenth lachrymose mistake.

Such creatures mostly have a human head,
which is a sort of comfort, looking down
at the tawny trunk, the quills of porcupine,
the rampant, iron tail of scorpion,
the scale-thick skin, those massive, velvet paws –
the sudden shock of knowing what we are,

all stitch-work crafted from fragmented parts,
the gentle and the violent juxtaposed,
the clue to skills so gothic that we lock
ourselves in villages with watch-tower clocks
and neighbours who take fright across the fields
at shadows falling from the fitful moon.

We think the self's Jerusalem the centre
of the world. Poor Travellers! Our broad earth
is various, skilful, only unexplored.
I know the Manticore will make us wise.
His many-bodied voice invites us enter
the dark labyrinth, not knowing the password.

Inside the Panopticon

The man who sits inside the hub is mad.
I merely have to cross my legs: he writes
it down. Not only are the walls of glass,
but each cell placed so his all-seeing eye
can pick out every gesture that I make,
each motion public, prayer or masturbation.

Even my own surface has grown vitreous,
my skin a crystal magnifying glass
through which he reads my hidden organs' thoughts
below the scrutiny of his bare bulb.
Laid naked in my shame, I play the game
of hide-and-seek with those whom I oppose.

Escape. I fix my mind on something sharp:
as if I turned a pane of glass end on
to disappear inside transparency.
I let this cutting edge bleed poison out
and draw blood curtains on the see-through walls.
I can make the prison go away.

I push glass splinters underneath my nails.
The pain can help disguise my exit route,
confuses him: his hounds of sheer pursuit
are hunting through my inner lacunae,
trying to sniff me out; they bay and root
among my synapses, their hot tongues red.

I have to multiply myself – my brave
lieutenants stand as sentries at the doors
which separate the segments of myself:
each one will vanish as he reaches it,
a small, imploding circle of deceit,
each sacrifice a gambit in the wars

the thread of who I am hangs from. No screw
on earth will take from me the needful art
which keeps my mind intact. I do not know
where all this ends because he must not too.
The first rule: being able to depart;
the next, forgetting where it is you go.

As Blue Light Slips Away

Looking up I see my daughter rest
her head on prayer hands
her body's mountain deepening
as blue light slips away.

Diabetes Today

I leaf through its latest issue as I wait
to be weighed, for eye tests, blood tests, urine samples,
low in the league table of hospital smells.
There's nothing lethal in my case to date

just warnings: 'smoking multiplies the risks;
your retina deteriorates; your feet
have lost their reflex – that's bad; I can treat
your illness but the odds are one in six

you'll reach retirement while you're still alive'.
Steve Redgrave, Gary Mabbutt are its heroes –
their stories seed beds where the message grows
that diabetics can live normal lives.

I've bitten through my tongue; come round at five
in piss-cold sheets; dislocated a hip;
crawled across filthy floors to split my lip
on toilet seats; been sightless when I drive.

I sit in waiting rooms and idly flick
through the small ads of our insignia:
insulin pens, white spirit, sharps, bizarre
chocolates, the nightmare of *the ribbed sock*.

Ghost in the Machine

Sometimes there is a sense of greyness close
as if you sat and stared down from a boat,
seeing the sky's reflection and the swish
of something else which might be seal or fish
or neither, just the shadow of the hull
among the polyps, or an Iceland gull
ghosting its lonely way from stack to stack.
There is no skill, no trick or subtle knack
to lend it form, abstract it from the sea,
dissect its flukes or, in captivity,
to make it balance beach balls on its nose.
The subject of another set of laws,
it fishes in the Sound uncertain things
the tide-wrack of the immaterial brings,
dreams of the underwater world, its eels
of strange ellipsis shocking you with tales
of sudden twists and undetected deeps,
the guardian of where the Kraken sleeps,
of coelacanth and serpent, squid and ray,
whose echo-soundings fade to waking day.
It is the force which shapes the minnow shoals,
which guides the drowning sailor to the whales.
It calibrates the sinking, icy weight
of water, keeps the course of currents straight.

You may have felt it lightly on your arm
just out of view, your boat facing the storm,

the water already raw, electric, clouds
boiling and bearing down. It was your guide.
Look how you learned to ride, run with the squall,
you who couldn't navigate at all.
Listen. If you wait long enough, you'll hear
a greyness like an ocean in your ear.

Reportage

Later, among the rubble roads of the suburbs
where already the broken slabs were being craned,
the iron rods uncased from them like ribs
– rebuilding was in the air, a kind of season –

I was allowed to meet a small huddle of children,
some of them mute and some merely silent
as if on parade, all with the same desiccated
exhalation coming from their throats.

After spending some time with them in a classroom
they began to speak words. They hadn't wanted it,
they were still small and only wanted to meet
their parents soon, please, or scream in the park.

Further in, where gutted windows raised their eyebrows
and whole streets were sealed in with a black tar,
others played jackstraws with the finger bones
on a sticky step. They lifted their shirts to scars

thin as their smiles. They made reloading actions,
rituals to ward off a *once-upon-a-time*
when they had filled schools with shouted insults
and lusted over labels they would have killed for.

More of it, more, they said, wiping the rainwater
from unblinking eyes, watching with disinterest
the cable men in trucks, the smiling orderlies
waiting at the street end to rope them together.

Nearer the centre silence had turned on itself.
Three small girls sat on a perfect lawn
as I joined them on the grass to wait, the sun
kindly warming the back of my old shirt.

Around midnight one said: *You were expected.*
What took you so long? Sit-down-and-then-move-on,
that's what you're called, or Come-to-count-the-dead;
your kindness isn't necessary here.

Her smile broke below unclouded eyes.
It grew into a knot around her neck.
Several small skulls watched from up a tree
as if expecting something more of me.

I kicked my heels with other journalists.
I filed my copy through the ears of stone.
I was alone with those I could not tell
about the city, which is everyone.

Sister

The one I never had lives inside me
ubiquitous as nematodes, their silver
parings slipping through my tissue, slivers
of moon, or ghosts that only I can see,
some dark cloud's lining. It's as if I hide
her beauty with my own peculiar mix:
all thumbs, bigfootedness, ruthless eclipse
of her in shadows of sororicide.

She tortures me to make me out as kind.
She knows I'm not but uses parallax
to blame me for the substance which she lacks.
In my body's darkness I can find
few virtues that her scorn cannot condemn
as cheap excuses typical of men.

Schubert

for Brian Redwood

It shocked me Schubert liked to lie all day
in bed with his huge wolfhound, Valkyrie,
and maybe Liz his girlfriend too. He'd play

violin in three orchestras on weekday evenings,
fiddle on Fridays in a scratch folk outfit and sing
too, sometimes. He had a talent for such things,

his house a shrine to mended instruments.
He'd stroke an *Amati* of doubtful provenance
to life to conjure me its resonance.

Sometimes he had to stash the shop sign when
the Revenue called up. He'd grin, his wine
silver in his hand, his thin lips carmine.

On Sundays he would shepherd me to the Lord
Napier to hear Bill Brunskill's Big Band, loud,
with smoky sixths and laid-back weekend crowds.

I was young then and London was a blur
of rain, demolished tower blocks and beer.
I spent the nights with him and Frank, a software

freak, saying how we'd died: Schubert at eight
lying in darkness, face to the wall, a blanket
of Hessian dyed to block the window out,

called back from the burning light by his dad,
to no sight or sound for several months; Frank dead
four minutes in a crash; all of us glad

to get a second chance, three of the 'twice-born'
talking away the extra time in Thorn-
ton Heath, waiting for the ordinary light of dawn.

Shields

Their pencilled outlines ghost the Borstal walls,
a breezeblock heraldry's half-written law
expressed in poster paints or Humbrol enamels,
the armorial achievements of the poor,

vaguely like hearts their chevron, chief, and pale,
painstakingly painted by a struggling hand
which tried too hard to keep things in control –
a wasted best on this escutcheoned island.

In the half-light they iridesce like stained glass.
The flaking plaster carries sable, gules,
tinctures of tar and blood, the brands of class
burned on the flesh of those who fault the rules.

Each one of them was loved and came to this:
a waste of labour filling up the hours,
a tiny cell decked out with bend and fesse,
a childhood, couped and gardant, behind bars,

their scope another kind of science, full
of argent, sinister, disordered forms,
the ordinaries of what is probable.
Such coats could never cleave nor keep them warm.

Charon

Your hand-bones click with each thick stroke
against the muscles of the tide.
Your empty face is turned aside
and hooded by a sackcloth cloak.
The skiff is caulked with creosote
which peels up like tiny hands.
The duck-boards where your tarsus stands
are knuckle-deep in grease. The boat
is rocking now against the quay,
grey as the dawn which is no dawn.
You stand aside to let me on.
What is it that you want with me?

No answer. Just these present threats.
Of course I want to run, but can't.
The steps go nowhere. I feel faint.
Strangely, I'm out of cigarettes.
The lip of earth on my toe-cap
is all I'll take to disembark
into the unforgiving dark.
Heart in my mouth, unready, I step
onto the Styx, into your sway.
I recognise your flinch from me –
that instinct at proximity.
I watch you row the world away.

Out on the slow reach nothing stirs.
The oars leave hints of whirlpools in
the sluggish tide like dimpled skin.

The water hangs from them as hairs
of long-dead bodies which have crossed.
These are the last tears I will cry.
They wash away my face and sigh
in the cold sea like something lost.
There is no coming back to shore.
Across the river children play
by chestnut trees. We edge away.
I think I should have loved you more.

Hoc est Corpus

Hocus-Pocus, the big-fisted conjuror,
who gave his stage name to a list of feats
longer than ribbons in his spangled sleeves,
who knew a bit about his audience,
for instance, just what it would swallow, swallowed
painted bird-eggs, then let linnets out
like gems between his fingers, freeing them
to the night sky. He had a gravitas
conveyed by heavy eyebrows, a confused look
and the habit of sighing slightly, mid-trick.

Those hands concealed as much as they revealed –
the mundane artifice of showmanship,
the hours designing cloths of gossamer
so subtle they could seem two things at once,
the way the brain can make a turning fan
turn backwards at another angle, or
conceal a slim girl in an old crone's face –
the stock-in-trade of journeyman magicians,
all of the tropes of magic hidden in
the raw material we call the world.

He could tell by touch the margin of error,
the rules which govern disbelief, the line
he trod each show between guffaws and awe.
His hands were bird-tables the audience ate off:
a point of honour just to feed them crumbs.
Such skill was arrogance, as all art is,

a light touch for a world where weight is grace.
He left them in the Twilight Zone between
a dream and things, offered them Heaven but
took care not to have to get them there.

He left that to others. The man himself
became a by-word for fakery and fraud,
the foolishness of spells. But here he is –
notice him bend, his neck glisten in torchlight,
his present and commanding rhetoric,
the dirt under his nails, the big stench
of his breath, his whole blaspheming circus.
They say it's hard to tell good stuff from bad.
Old Hocus will allow the difference
and make it disappear in his huge hands.

Cartographers

Children in the back lane making maps
without quadrant, compass or theodolite.
They are peopling the globe, geodesists
of limitless scope who do not record their findings,
just call the readings out like antiphons:

'Beyond the hedge are weeds which steal your soul.'
'This washing-line makes you invisible.
The pegs are swallows bringing messages.'
'This bush is where the gibbets mop and mow.'
'A paddle marks the place the ship was wrecked.'

They say there is a world behind our own,
a *Terra Nova*, shimmering and shy:
the lane, its five-pace width an estuary
of nettle forests, rusty tyre-track pools
where dragons breed the colour of the sun.

Their voices drift into the dark kitchen
where I allow the lane its true projection –
their pictures forming on the artex walls;
the work of countless children calling down
the future, its unmapped co-ordinates.

Whale Bone

I found it half submerged in shallow swell
off Uist, big as a dinner plate, on one
side smoothish, small ridged rings spiralling
into a lumpy eye, the other like
a shocked Medusa, matted locks flayed out
like coral from a central hub. It smelled
for days, but I still carried it about
asking the island's elders what it was.
They shrugged and balanced it on sea-rough hands.
They said they'd never seen the like. I caught
in their eyes the awe at what the sea throws up.

An ornament it sits now in my study
smelling still (now chalk, now bone-clay), rutted
surface like a damaged nail, dense
with knots and cauls like storms which scour the sea
to ragged blades. I rest it on my palm,
imagining the silk-weight as I slip
in ecstasy between the thunderous waves.

Tenure

It must be magnetism of the soul
the way a needle in me points to you,
a rising sea-wind cracking my cagoule,
the black slabs glistening in the smirr, the view
astern of churning waters. We skirt Mull
and leave behind what seems the furthest shore,
a smudge of shadow with its frieze of gulls,
setting our outward course for Eigneig Mhor,
an inward space the arctic current feeds,
an exile's red carpet, the unforgiving sea
and lonely Kyles as much home as I need
as giants' arms of rock reach out for me.

So many times: two summers under ten –
the first fix – then I couldn't get enough.
Four months at Dyce learning to get drinks in,
to ken myself in whatever mirror, to love
the back of women's knees and Aberdeen rowies;
my first Minch-crossing out to Stornoway
with John Dodds in his Ford Capri as Bowie's
Aladdin Sane boomed out and glens flashed by;
camping at Kirvik where we once were saved
by a crofter who searched our tent for *a partition*
because he was concerned how we'd behave,
me and the two French girls. He found none
but still let us camp, fed us pancakes, scones.
Summers of rain on bikes; orchids and clovers
whispering beside the bittern-booming ocean;
abandoned walls at Ormiclate; long hours

shut in your wood museums, their photographs
of every islander, your history
of dispossessions, cruelty and griefs;
always the wind, always your light's clemency.

The ferry circles in Loch Maddy Sound.
The threadbare hills glister in the sun
after sudden rain. My feet will touch the ground,
blessed, I will call it, as I am joined again.
I listen to the ghosts tell what was lost:
poor crofts, Atlantic rocks and breakers lie
along the spun-out cloth of ragged coasts,
dubh lochans laid down under dead grey skies,
the wire wool of the wind on the soul; such
beauty and emptiness. On Bosta sands,
the worthless gold sifts slowly from my hands.

But if it seems like I presume too much,
Scotland, then picture me by the wee caravan
at Stoer, racing my plastic boats which sing
on the glass braids of the burn brown with peat
or climbing Quinnaig in cloud, staring
down at the quartz diamonds round my feet.

Roderick the Imposter

The prophet was not entirely without honour.
He was well-liked, well-proportioned, flame-haired,
dexterous as any on the cliffs, unlettered
not unintelligent. He claimed he'd heard

John the Baptist in Gaelic by Mullach Sgar.
The apparition wore a cloak and hat
like a Sassenach. As visions mostly do
it spoke out of a bush – and told him what

a women had to do for easy births,
how to sing a husband's want to sleep
and save a self for holiness. It gave him
sermons, on how the bush made quick the kelp;

how cattle should not eat of it because
it was God's Word. This much was without harm.
Then several women of the island spoke
of lewd acts which he had performed with them.

We listened hard for weeks as, one by one,
they testified their multitudes of shame
in tears, twisting their hair in their chapped hands.
I wrote down every fallen woman's name.

They shipped him off St Kilda one summer dawn,
the girlish faces gathered in a shrinking knot.
The last he saw of them. He went quietly
to a Skye dungeon where they let him rot.

He said he hadn't understood a word
of what was spoken in his head: it flummoxed
him. He only cleared his mind of self
and let himself be carried by the text.

The women gave themselves freely to him –
he would instruct them in the liturgies
and other forms of heavenly intercourse.
He mounted them to make quick their bodies

dark, infernal, dead without his gift.
If they agreed, he said they needn't die,
but be transported into ornament
on Palominos, clothed in organdie,

would ride the ether westwards straight to God.
On ragged cliffs in twos they bent their necks
to his touch, stepping clean out of their skins
in ecstasy above the naked rocks.

The Seal People

I had watched them far off in the rough skerries,
their long cries carried to land on spindrift,
their bodies slipping like soap between the white
knuckles of waves, vanishing in the rip
for dives of joy into the great grey acres.

It was luck itself to find them there that day –
their visits rare and those who saw them blessed.
Alone, as the sun glared briefly over Heskair
making them dark as dolphins, I waited here
on the machair until they came ashore. Then

they skinned themselves assuming human shape,
their seal-natures pulled up on the sand
like boats beyond the breakers' reach and roar
and built a beacon out of tidewrack where
they cooked the fish they carried in their tails.

I only know that they were beautiful,
their foreheads spangled with salt, their eyes like pairs
of moons, their bodies glistening like gods'.
They looked at me, their faces filled with distance,
the scope of journeys sketched in their high cheeks.

A shiver takes you when your soul is moved.
That night I shook myself to somewhere else.
They showed me how to talk with just my hands;
how I could leave my body like a pelt
on the cold sand and watch it from above;

how they had swum the margins of the world
trailing their fingers in the edgy sea
as if they drew a human envelope
in water, reaching out around us with
a hand to mark the limits of our kind.

They came from where the ice and water meet:
I saw the islands long untenanted,
the far, stark dwellings they had left behind
for the dark, forgetting ocean, with its freedom.
They clothed themselves again at break of day,

departing from our world on the high crests
of surf, their arms describing arcs of spray,
their laughter tumbling back on skeins of wind
to where I watched, diminishing. Their name
meant 'us' as all the names of peoples do.

Loanwords

There ought to be a fine for not returning them.
My grandma left me some
which stick with me like fruit gums on a seat –
a *thunderplump*, us *poor, wee starvin' craturs*;
her non-negotiable *ne'er cast a clout*;
injunctions not to *coggle* on a chair.

In her deteriorated Aberdonian
she initiated us in all things Scotch –
the indignities of whisky,
the drab doctrines of an unenlightened Kirk,
the whole rigmarole of tartan blethers.
She paraded the clan ptarmigan brooch.

Eau de Cologne staved off the smell of age.
I used to sit and listen in the fug
to her life-musings: her sister who had achieved
a saint's status through a life committed
to embroidery and a sharp tongue;
ubiquitous brother farmers; her brief fling

in an art studio; how I *mustnae dream*
to steal a woman off another man
and something warm and weak like plaid running
through the family she traced from Bannockburn,
all of whom I felt were present when
she wheeled in circles round her theme.

Her heirloom was the girdle, black with centuries
of fat, on which she used to bake drop-scones,
those liquid rings of light which burnt to bronze,
at Strachan, then Nether Benholm, Fontainbleu
in the blitz, at Syddall Avenue
and now a terrace in a town near Leeds.

When grandma died there was no coronach,
just the glide of velvet funeral drapes,
muzak of piped pipes,
a thin ghost of smoke from the furnace chimney
which smelled strangely like her talc,
and settled, couthy in the cemetery.

Some new and recent poetry from Anvil

GAVIN BANTOCK
Just Think of It

OLIVER BERNARD
Verse &c.

NINA BOGIN
The Winter Orchards

NINA CASSIAN
Take My Word for It

PETER DALE
Under the Breath

DICK DAVIS
Belonging

HARRY GUEST
A Puzzling Harvest
COLLECTED POEMS 1955–2000

MICHAEL HAMBURGER
From a Diary of Non-Events

JAMES HARPUR
Oracle Bones

PHILIP HOLMES
Lighting the Steps

ANTHONY HOWELL
Selected Poems

MARIUS KOCIEJOWSKI
Music's Bride

PETER LEVI
Viriditas

GABRIEL LEVIN
Ostraca

E A MARKHAM
A Rough Climate

THOMAS McCARTHY
Mr Dineen's Careful Parade

DENNIS O'DRISCOLL
Exemplary Damages

SALLY PURCELL
Collected Poems

GRETA STODDART
At Home in the Dark

DANIEL WEISSBORT
Letters to Ted